The Purple Sun

*A Poetic Journey Through
Domestic Violence*

Lori Jean Finnila

Copyright 2024 Lori Jean Finnila, Portland, OR
Library of Congress Control Number: 2024921536

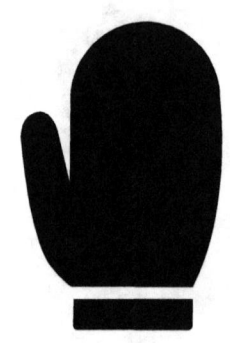

Foreward

This is my journey and many others from domestic violence as the definition began to get so twisted I couldn't find a name for it. I couldn't relate to what it ended up appearing to be where I didn't know enough about human trafficking. I learned so many bad things can be done with no one's control it would seem yet so many in control seemed to hold the strings to my freedom, if not helping toward toward my abuse.

Sadly I met many along the way hurt very badly in so many forms of abuse in the same position as myself and found how connected abuse is coming from so many circumstances yet all sitting in the same place as me. The form of retaliation on them didn't have to be the exact same as mine to relate and feel a connection and feel empathy. This is a lot of what these poems are about in this book. Please take in its importance and I hope to shed hope onto the world.

'Dedicated to God who has been beside me my entire journey.'

The Truth of Love and Hate

I'm up at my makeup table writing perhaps for the first time as I reveal the truth in my story - the truth of love and hate. The truth of pain on unwanted children, as it comes so close to me through domestic violence. The truth of revenge and retaliation that broadens the word domestic violence into potential human trafficking upon a woman who would jump in front of classmates when bullied.

It came upon a woman who as a young girl could only see fit to stop pain to others' when it came her way, no matter the consequences, when she was left with a cracked front tooth from a punch from a boy when her friend was bullied when in elementary school when she stepped in as she met so many other brave women along the way that will and have done the same.

It brings the meaning of abuse to a new level connecting all levels of abuse through greed, retaliation, anger, and control. Many don't realize, I feel, or ignore, how much pain and suffering in so many forms and so easily done is inflicted on those that step out, aside, and beyond social forms of the horrors of the forms of abuse to share that are put upon them for us, whether it is meant to be a threat or fully blown into another area of crime used as punishment for retaliation.

This is my story to be told for God as he saved my life from all this, as I've seen so many suffer that need our help that I will not leave behind.

It appears as so many seem marketed in a society with no feeling. There are ones who are distanced from love to stand out easier to be marketed for someone to stay *alive or be pleased. Such a cold, cold world we live in.*

But those able that are strong enough learn to live and bring life to some victims that never would ordinarily have life anymore, hopefully bringing in no more pain.

The Purple Sun Opens

Another land,   time place

another dark scary   door

God shines the sun down on this green leaf for me to see

changing it to the color of purple of the symbol of domestic violence. I couldn't see its importance at the time though growing up I saw the dreaded abuse upon my mother leaving me in a dark scary place feeling no way of communication. I was destined to this as well in life.

I lost her when running from abuse myself never being able to see her funeral where I felt she died from her abuse.

I don't see the purple leaf's full importance until much later.

It carries to a tunnel

I'm not afraid

I'm stepping in

the green leaf that has its color changed

I feel now is for me to see

to see its importance, significance

to this important journey to be told

with my gifts that I've been given

as well as a life survived to do this

all from God

Last night it signified to me

when I had cried in pain

as the blood flowed from me

when I asked God to take me from this pain

at that moment that I couldn't bare

he replied to tell the story

of what's going on as he saved me

As the beginning of this poem

came to me later

that I didn't remember that I wrote

or how it came about

it's at these times that I realize

it's from God

It's so important to understand and be told the meaning of truth and hate.

Table of Contents

- 5. Forward
- 9. The Truth of Love and Hate
- 12. The Purple Sun
- 21. My Prince
- 23. Women Who Have Courage To Die For Their Dreams
- 26. Flowers In The Dark
- 28. Someone Will Hear Your Intelligent Words
- 30. Hit On the Head
- 32. Confidence
- 33. Clear
- 35. A Bitchin' Girl
- 37. Divine Breath
- 39. God Please Let Me Wake Up Tomorrow
- 42. I Ride My Ship
- 44. I Pray That My Hands Are Clean
- 46. I Feel Blessed

48.	I Thought I Needed Love To Be Beautiful
50.	Leaves Falling
51.	I Was Meant To Be Beautiful
53.	Living In the Sun
54.	Roses
56.	Survival
58.	Strong Girl
61.	Never Knew
64.	Pretty Little Ornament
68.	My Small Place
71.	My Angel
72.	Slap
74.	So Sad At One Time
77.	The Violin Bleeds
78.	The Wings Are Made and Begin To Fly
79.	Beautiful Flutes That I Want To Write To
80.	When They Pass
81.	Savourable Time
83.	My Starfish
86.	No More Beauty Than This

88. *Waste Of Time*
89. *The Goat's Bell*
92. *Your Girl Hiding Around the Corner*
94. *Distractions*
96. *Making Dreams*
97. *Women Who Have Courage To Die For Their Dreams (cont.)*
103. *I Will Be Receiving a Long Awaited Feeling Of Love*
105. *Closing*

My Prince

Aah my prince son of Abraham
where are you now
what is your value now to others, society?
You are still a prince to me

I have worked so long
to be ready
for your carpet
to come my way
with your thick, black hair
swaying turning me on
waiting for your long
thick, strong arms
to comfort me

My wish to this fate as I stand still
glazed in my eyes to a dream state
all the time of a life of beauty and magic
this has kept me going locked in a closet

How dreams are so close to the imagination

as the sand in the pyramids

that I now watch cascade

from my makeup table

in a piece of sand art

as I put on my face to cover my marks

My sand, my place, my prince

making his journey along the sand to me

like rushing waves of water

the power of the sea

that I am amazed with

we won't bend for anyone.

Women Who Have Courage To Die For Their Dreams

Life is still becoming
more fresher and fresher
I wonder when this will stop
how much fresh can we have
I still bring newness in

Finally grateful
after feeling death for so long
I feel peeks of life more now
as though to toy with me
but lovingly
what is it trying to tell me?

I know there's more to know
but gratefulness is taking on
an unfamiliar meaning to me
I feel my body more
but through my head

is this good?

Am I closer to death
or becoming more alive?
Is this around me
so important to life

Or am I learning the meaning of it
and accepting another life?
I want to be all this
sipping it in like the richest of feelings

It's always in the early morning
yet late at night too when I struggle
struggle to stay alive it seems
but it could be
just challenges in life
all is quiet when it happens

I wonder if anyone is around
to help me or witness this?

Nope, I am all alone

perhaps this is meant to be at this time.

Flowers In The Dark

*Through the castles on sacred land
many cries we've heard from so long ago*

*So light deep down buried
so surreal far away
into another land, time, place
another dark, scary door
That opens and carries
into the same tunnel*

*Some are locked in somewhere inside
they need peace, courage, and love
to go to heaven
to spread the word to stop the persecution
all the way to our ancient mothers*

*Many women gather
many women who speak are beaten
those that know the women's cry*

are our answer
how we will survive

The sadness of their loss
the world needs to know
dark and cold
so cold so deep
too deep to mention

360 to today
the cries are the same
I still hear them from the far away lands
as I had so many times when I was younger
the flowers in the dark
that cry to go to heaven.

Someone Will Hear Your Intelligent Words

Even as your hiding

Even in the dark

Walking around corners

So far from everyone

As you dodge in and out

throughout your day

waiting for the chance

to speak in the night

for no one else to hear

She is there

far away

dark and cold

The Purple Sun — Lori Jean Finnila

so cold, so deep, so light

deep down buried

The sun shines so yellow

fills the sky

2 skies that fold

1 an unknown place

so surreal far away into another land

into another land

someone will hear

your intelligent words.

Hit On The Head

My nose is gruffled
from the thick air
I'm feeling dizzy

I'm coughing
thinking I'm losing my mind

I'm remembering things years ago
like they're yesterday
not sure of their proper time frame
It dawns-my hit on the head-but it can't be
because it doesn't seem practical

Aaah I'm thinking clear now
it was the mold in the apartment
I hear it takes your brain

Oh I have to fix this
I will

Just a crack in the window
I'm feeling better
I'm thinking clearer
I'm still getting flashes of my life
I can't line up the times to
Oh that's right
I was hit on the head.

Confidence

*Is confidence built around others' views
of my entirety that surrounds me
Do I have to try it all myself to know
or lear what everyone says has value*

*Can I walk out my door
with half of what others already know
and half of what I know and feel confident
I've lived enough of life
to be lifted high enough
to feel the ultimate of me?*

Clear

I'm feeling clear
I'm where I've wanted to be for so long
It seems like it came to me magically
but I've been working for it for many years

How can many years seem lucky
why does it take so long to get to magic?

Perhaps it's the magic in the sky
the lands, sea, sun, and moon
we have no control over

Perhaps it's destiny
and we have just arrived
should we welcomingly be open to it

Are we safe
is this really a happy thing?

All I know is the bottom of my stomach
isn't as thick in a pit
my muscles are more elastic
I can move my limbs
I will take this as a sign
of opportunity and go with it.

A Bitchin' Girl

Whoops a broken bone again
can't use my arms
can't use my hands
my legs hurt

But I'm gonna get back on that ride
I know I can do it again
It just hurts for a short while
I know I can heal to do it one more time

I get apprehensive too
but I want to keep my body going
don't want to sag
don't want to get scared of myself in the mirror

Want to think long
longer than I do now
why do I think I can do all these things

and not hurt myself enough
to not be able to get back up again

I'm just a crazy girl
a crazy little girl it seems
in society's view
she sees her sexy reflection
no matter what the truth is

She's just a crazy girl
who loves herself too much
to face the world as she should

I'm not who I was 20 years ago
my mind doesn't relate to this theme though
I forget to check my steps
watch every move I make
to not break a bone again
but I'm still a bitchin' girl!

Divine Breath

I'm gonna fight thru the pain
through the agony I identify
I make controversy with
right before I feel to pass out

The rotting body
I refuse to watch go that way
I ride through the asylum
even if I leave my divine breath
I know I'm going somewhere better
I'll ride through my divine breath
to surpass to thrive from where I am
I'm fighting my crumbling body
that no one can see but me

Only I know the blurry view
and uncertain days
that lay ahead for me

needing a miracle to heal
from all the abuse
I'll feel the presence
of all those above me
that did the same

I'll be the healer
for those that don't know life
I'll heal myself
even if it's an everyday thing.

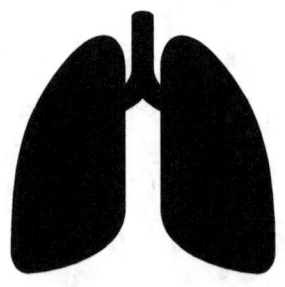

God Please Let Me Wake Up Tomorrow

My mind goes when I need help
I have to take something that affects me like a
child now

I fight many wars with many people
here I go down again
please God let me wake
tomorrow morning

I take the gold liquid
I now poke with a pin
to make sure I don't get too much
in my body from the pill
it can take me down so badly
especially after that crash on my head
into the shelves
while going into the closet mirror
I so shouldn't have done that

I could feel my head
get sucked in
or was it just an illusion
please God
let me wake up tomorrow morning

My body is in so much pain now
from the effects of abuse
I need help from my liquid gold
in a hemp pill
that makes my mind like a child
get lost one more time

One for the pain
and many other different pills for energy
to follow as they collide in my body
I have one more day I can get through
but with a brain injury I can't think straight

I'm taken down to a state
I know I have no control over

The Purple Sun — Lori Jean Finnila

*I don't know if I'll be lucky enough
to wake up this coming morning*

*As I surrender
I feel my mind go to a place of peace
feeling I might be lucky this time again
to my fate again to wake up one more time
God please let me wake up tomorrow
morning.*

I Ride My Ship

*I ride my ship
dashing forward
I'm a leader of my mission
I stand at the head of my boat*

*My eyes are stern, intense
what's to come about
that I am about to undertake*

*I waste not every bite of food I consume
peering at its minimal existence in question
I will fight here to remain*

*No loud sounds will you hear from me
only the intent of my journey
at its highest you will see.*

The Purple Sun   Lori Jean Finnila

I Pray That My Hands Are Clean

I pray that my hands are clean
the soap behind my ears
has done the job
my private smells perfect

I pray I've curled my hair right
it shines and flows in the sunlight
it's soft to the touch
it brings joy to everyone

I pray my attire is of satisfaction
not too tight around the rear
no underwear lines for everyone to see

I pray I speak well at the table
or not at all
make the face
that will make the church proud

The Purple Sun — Lori Jean Finnila

I pray I eat all my peas
And never throw them away again
walk with a long grazingly slope
not turn too fast

I pray I can sit up tight long enough
as I ache in my heart
That it won't show
in front of the ones I love
that I try so hard to impress
to get through my dreary female life.

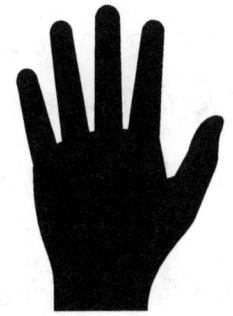

I Feel Blessed

I feel blessed when I have
fresh vegetables in the house
I was able to get out to get them
I was able to buy them because
I got them at a good price
I feel blessed when their color looks healthy
It reminds me of when I was young
The taste of fresh squash
from the stand down the road
I would ride my bike to and pay a nickel for

The man trusted me to go through
and choose the biggest one if I wanted
all I had to do is put the nickel in the basket

He was near in the field picking
more vegetables and smiling at me
he trusted me
I was surprised

The Purple Sun — Lori Jean Finnila

I asked him if it was ok
to touch the vegetables before I did
he said 'yes'

I said 'you trust me?'
and he said 'yes'
I wondered if I had a new friend
but he let me know that wasn't it

I would go home and boil the squash
until it was almost like mush-I loved it that way
then when it was done and I'd put it in my
bowl-which always had a little water still left in
it from the squash, I hated that
this would always happen and make the loads
of butter I put on it more weak tasting yet I
could still taste the seeds-I loved this, they
would be just a little firm,
I'd mush it more.

I Thought I Needed Love To Be Beautiful

*I used to be so pretty
then one day it went away
I could hardly see myself
I lost myself*

*When I lost my looks
I couldn't believe it
It came on strong with a blow
Then took me down slowly
with so many more
some just alike
I didn't know who I was*

*Then one day it came back
The happiness I feel
I can't be thankful enough
I skip like a little girl
and twirl in my shoes*

The Purple Sun   Lori Jean Finnila

The girl I once knew
I'll never take advantage again
of the beauty I now have back
all over my body and within

All I need is what I feel
I'll never feel I need love
from someone else
to feel pretty again.

Leaves Falling

*My life is like leaves falling
everyone I'm running to catch
losing my breath
tiring one more day*

*Though I love the progression
I feel the need to run
and catch the leaves anyway.*

I Was Meant To Be Beautiful

I'm shedding my skin
I'm not resisting
I'm embracing the change ahead
It wouldn't be wise I feel to do this
I'm accepting the new change in me

I must accept my path that has led me here
to this place to see this change
grab it, grow, recognize and embrace it
it is good

Change is good
it has to happen
when you fight for good
or you can't get past bad
It feels unfamiliar and unsure
it can be scary
but I've made so much change already

all I have to do is grab the security to me
that I know will happen going forward

My change is extreme and drastic
as mountains and storms are
but this is my fate
and I have to accept it
I want to get to the good
that's coming at me

I'll fall into it like the caterpillar
coming out of its shell
I was meant to fly and be beautiful
I won't miss this chance again
I will watch the beautiful transformation
of me happening.

Living In The Sun

I'm stepping into unchartered territories
but doing it for the better of the world
I have no idea how it will turn out
but I'm so looking forward to living in the sun

I've come so far
I know I need to keep seeing this
as I walk into a part of the world I don't know
I will relish what I will: see, touch, taste, feel,
hear, smell
the air feels so much more open.

Roses

Roses keep coming to me

I connect to them in a wash

I feel them in a lotion

I see the word

in my reading unexpected

I picture red roses

in a row on a dress

I see them in something I carry

next to my breast

I picture a rose in my camera lens

as I look back at it

waiting for it to set onto words

that are waiting for its picture in my book.

The Purple Sun   Lori Jean Finnila

Survival

Trauma book hmmmm……..
no vendettas but still wrote from pain
seeking humanity you recorded
how it's related to your survival

Where was I inside this process?
What was happening with me?
Did I recognize what was happening?
What change did I make
to make myself a hero?
It's about how you make of what happened
and not what happened
what we believe, think, or feel
after all that has been done

A lot of trauma survivors shut down
which is ok
to have no feelings

The Purple Sun — Lori Jean Finnila

to illustrate a book
metaphor or speculation?

Address the reader's needs
with different emotions
call out how hard it is to write the book
I don't want to talk about it
there are no words for this moment

When you have no more books to write
after this one: gap-look, info gaps,
research, journal more feelings
or I felt nothing again
Changes of how you feel years passed
writing the book
meeting reader's needs
it ends up being for the public, not you.

Strong Girl

Though you may have second-guessed yourself
thought you could never come as far as you are

You made that change
that change that was life curdling
but had to be made

These changes are never easy
they are the last thought
to the mind of ever doing
the hardest things to do

the hardest things to do
are the best for us

You can't see it fully

even in the honesty of the situation
even knowing at that moment
that this needs to be done
though I see it now
way past this moment
so I can pass this on

You see the changes
when you're at peace and say huh?
you can't understand
how that peaceful moment came
and relates to this one
or how it ever came
starting out only for a few seconds

You have to rethink the obvious
of what you've done
that brought you to this place
it's so surreal
that you know you can never
add this feeling up again

*But now you have the wisdom
to know you can
the journey you have to take
when you need to feel peace again
to find this place
you strong girl.*

Never Knew

I never knew life could be so hard
no one ever told me how it is to be a woman
and to be all alone

I left you cause I couldn't stand
getting hit by you
it was enough
even if only once or twice
in different ways
that you may not perceived
as hitting
to make me leave

I never knew life
could be so hard

I had it all

I was safe and loved before this
I felt at one time
I knew now I was doing the right thing
I wanted it again somehow, somewhere

Life grabbed me so hard
I couldn't get away
I was told I should have left well enough alone
but I thought I could have it all

Please come back to me
that feeling of security
tell me I don't have to feel this anymore
to be a woman and be free
I just want to feel the love
I once had without any judgment
after leaving now with no more respect.

The Purple Sun   Lori Jean Finnila

Pretty Little Ornament

*I was a pretty little ornament frustrated
waiting to bust out onto the outside
I had so much movement in my body
and brain in my mind
that I wasn't allowed to use*

*I had a hard time sitting there looking pretty
which I was sent out to do so many times
in my new jobs now in New York City
as a twenty-something year old*

*I had a job from the past
that tried to set me up
as a human trafficking victim
making me look like a troubled juvenile
coming from a broken home*

The Purple Sun   Lori Jean Finnila

My mind would seep this in
at some jobs later
when I was at my highest
in the Fortune 500 world

I was bad at typing in school
I could barely keep my mind on the keys
it would have rather
I kept my mind on the bad boy
that wanted nothing good for me

I wasn't allowed to talk
to the guidance counselor
at school about college
it was said that my father
that I found out was not
said a lot of bad things about me
I couldn't go to anyone else in the there
I ended up with a counselor
outside of there instead
that set me up to have

*after hushing me, drugging me, and telling me
to 'shut up' as I hemorrhaged after
unknowingly, to having my unborn baby killed*

*The bad boy that would insist
picking me up to bring me to school
I already suffered black and blue from
would take me in late many times
I was punished more than him by the school
football coach*

*I was congratulated after all this
from the high school principal
for being able to win all I ever wanted
walking next to the abusive man
I now married felt I had to marry.*

The Purple Sun — Lori Jean Finnila

My Small Place

I'm in a small place
so small and closed-in
but I appreciate the space where I have all my favorite things
and how pretty it is

Sometimes I worry
when I can't breathe right
I know it's because of this small space
and being forced in tight quarters growing up
but I comfort myself
telling myself it will be alright

It will be alright in this small space

The Purple Sun — Lori Jean Finnila

because it has love, warmth,
and most importantly necessities
I look around at my pots and pans
all lined up on shelves

My counter corners cleaned
and stacked with my salt, peppers,
sponges and dish soap
necessities are important
the most important I think

Fear shouldn't be underweighted to this
it should be more important shouldn't it?
I need many things
this should not come first, no?

If I didn't have this small space
I wouldn't have saved money
to make it to the doctors
have fresh vegetables
and money to buy milk

to make my much needed yogurt
for my sick stomach
the expensive turmeric for my ginger tea
that rests my mind and body
from anxiety in my digestion
many tissues that are so expensive
to dry my tears

I take in as much oxygen as I can daily
thinly through a straw-like motion
to aerify myself
this brings my thinking brain back
enough to appreciate this small space

And don't worry about tomorrow
I tell myself
it has a mind of its own
and at its own time and place.

My Angel

I still think of you
your body before me
I caress you consoling you after
I felt you kick and you were taken
away
or is it loving you I'm not sure

You were taken from me
when I was so young
I thought I knew what abuse was
until this day

I still can't fathom this
how anyone could do this to you or I
I picture your face
but I can only imagine
I will fight for other children.

Slap

I heard
I feel
the slap
I can't figure out
which, where the noise

seems more relevant

My high esteem seems unimportant
where am I fighting for my life?

Did I say something to offend you
did I step on your toes
speak out of line
not return the borrowed book from the library

Perhaps I saluted your mother or father wrong
wore my hat in the wrong direction

The Purple Sun — Lori Jean Finnila

wore blue eye shadow

Maybe I was late for work
turned my back too much
wanted too much
or dreamed too much
but what does that have to do with you?

Next time I'll spray you full force with the hose
throw your favorite things out so far down
they'll never be of value again
make sure I don't give you a smile
wear steel and bring my hammer.

So Sad At One Time

I know why I've been so sad at one time

I know

but you always say you're sorry later

as long as you don't throw me out

that would hurt me

One of my thoughts of a best friend

who was an alcoholic

that locked me in the house

then dropped me off at a truck stop with a quarter to make a phone call

of course I could only rely

on the truck drivers there

The truck driver wanted me to go in the back

when I wouldn't he threw me out onto the highway

I ran to a hotel that took me in

This was all after

my boyfriend smashed my head

on his brand new SUV window

and left me sleeping on the floor

of his empty apartment with curtains left

from a window to wrap in that kept me warm

that led me to here

Not before my brother put me in an abandoned apartment he managed with water damage on the floor

I was now made to sleep on

next to this same ex boyfriend

who just beat me the night before.

The Violin Bleeds

*To the approach, emotions
like green entwines with the depth of nature
jiving, a presumption ruling out philosophy
and the beauty to meaning*

*Fresh and flourishing
those unknown coil to the meaning
because of the room that has music
and is universal to everyone
the violin bleeds.*

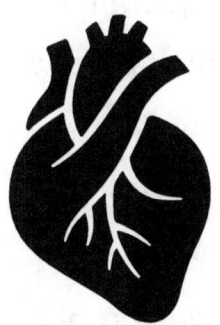

The Wings Are Made and Begin to Fly

Learning to love the body
once traumatized
running so many years
to be able to reflect temporarily
astonishment and power
creating a constant change
coming to terms
with marks up and down vertically

it lays back so eloquently
now creating a constant change
in physicality
like in a book of myths
right before the eyes
the wings are made and begin to fly.

Beautiful Flutes That I Want To Write To

Beautiful flutes that keep me up

the sound that keeps my mind inspired

dancing with beautiful feelings

the secret to magic and mystery

sparkling air like in church

God singing the choir.

When They Pass

Love is sad when it's not with us

love is sad when that person has gone

love is sad when we don't feel them with us

but if we keep them in our hearts

they are in the same space

though we might not feel them

or see them

or have them

right next to us in any way

we can be sure they are around us

as everyone else is when they pass.

Savourable Time

I will make the time succulent,

dreamy, untouchable, unseen

unfelt, unheard of

for me

I will fly high

all alone

and fear the sky

from inside

I will dodge the stingrays

and love the starfish

as I love the water too - I learned to make this place my salvation very young

in such a hard world

Pain and fear

may be less relevant

to this time

and space

I have on this earth.

My Starfish

*Beauty that is beautiful
even if it's not perfect
Beauty distorted on purpose
to show new beauty
a home is being made in the mind
people and their opinions
are so scattered about*

*My dreams are close
I can see the ocean and feel its breeze
my life is opening to me
with its hands
reaching wide
My eyes, head, ears, are receiving
receiving a long awaited feeling
of love and confidence
with years of independence
to a second childhood*

The flying starfish
move for me my friend
I'm an outcast
life hasn't turned out like I planned

As the sand cascades
like magic rushes of water
equal to the power of the sea
movement I have no control over

Newly learned with you beside me
move for me my starfish
my marks, my internal wounds
long term affects need help to my body

Move for me starfish
as she lays back
sleeping so eloquently
that's all she can do
holding her hand herself
moving beautifully as she once knew

The Purple Sun — Lori Jean Finnila

Learning to love herself
receiving a long awaited feeling
of love and confidence outside of herself

Yes you will get that second glance
at these circumstances
feeling the shrill
of the essential central decline being uplifted.

No More Beauty Than This

Your head lays on the bed

Your beautiful eyes shine in the light

so soft so glowing

your face, your look so serene

coming at me

Everything you are right now

I can mold you into a statue in my mind

and see it everyday

You never have to move

it's all I want to see

and I'll be perfectly happy

If you ever do move I'll be lost

how will I get through my day

how will I get through my life
if you moved out of my view

I know at some point you have to
but I will hold the outline of you
your contour in my mind
for my day the rest of my life
and wait for this moment again.

Waste Of Time

It's never a waste   of time
to drink a cup of tea
take your time swallowing it
tasting it
sitting down
while you're drinking it

It's never a waste of time
to sit and do nothing
to wait for the sign
of what to do next
to hear someone else's meaning of life
to take in a moment
and feel an empathetic reaction.

The Goat's Bell

The secret to magic and mystery

the goat's bell

I so remember

as I so desperately held for comfort

as I was kept in my room so often

Flutes I love that I want to write to

precious sound that keeps my mind inspired

dancing with beautiful feelings

remembering all the gold I was taught to look for

that was also on my darling play tea cup set just for me that I was only allowed to play with when I come to this place

The look on your face my half sister, or aunt? not sure which if even, that kept me going

I can't imagine the pain I suffered

that you seemed to know when I was the black sheep of the family

or a mess when I needed school lunch or clothes

when I looked too thin on Flag Day

as you cried in the background

and remembering now

from all that I learned what love is from you.

Your Girl Hiding Around the Corner

I don't know where you want me to touch
I don't know where your sensors are
I imagine a man doesn't like the neck
the arms, wrists, toes

I want to see your smile
when I approach
what I'll do for this
I'm not sure
please tell me
give me a hint
I dream our love
as we dance
turn together
the steps are so far in my mind
how do I find forever
your girl hiding around the corner.

The Purple Sun   Lori Jean Finnila

Distractions

Not knowing your state of mind
leaves you in limbo
not being able to hold onto anything steadily
or physically
leaves a place with no answers

A place of choice
where there's no known outcome

But the outcome
to a chance of happiness
made through a choice of freedom
not only do you not know the outcome to
but others don't either

One good thing about this is
when others don't know
they can't stop you from your outcomes
your beauty that comes out is true to you

with no distractions.

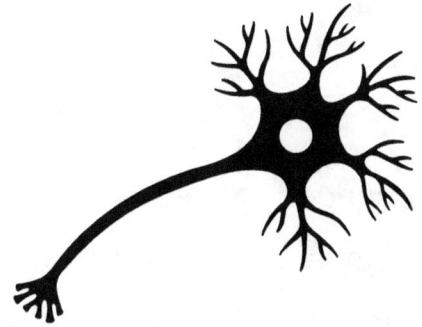

Making Dreams

Controlling confidence
making dreams
dreams happening
controlling fears
reaching out

controlling changes
accepting change
making change.

Women Who Have Courage To Die For Their Dreams (continued)

*I think of my last day as I know of it
how surreal and close the sounds will be
how close the sounds once were
I can't help but think of this day a lot
reflecting on the past*

*I know now how close it is to me
and I can see how fast time flies
because of this we can't stop it
all we can do is fill it up
with as much life as possible to make it longer
Length brings me hope, excitement
happiness to a fuller life*

*beauty that is beautiful
even if it's not perfect*

*Beauty in the eye of the beholder
brings much relief
there is hope for all
we are all special*

*Beauty that is distorted on purpose
to show meaning
new beauty, a new meaning to beauty
a new purpose to this beauty*

*New originalities are introduced
perhaps to extend humanity in time
of so much hope needed
as we continue this cycle*

*New forms of life are introduced showing the
strength in the freshness of the natural-all
things natural take over as people awaitingly*

with their scattered opinions let it take over
prominently, pleasantly, reassuringly

I will be visiting the water
so surreal as it will be
in its beauty and totally
alone out of my comfort zone

As I would feel the end of my days
not really knowing the comparison
but so perfect as it would be
so out of my control where I need to be

My hope is to have happiness
a happiness that only this place can give
a happiness out of my control
where the most happiness is
where I don't feel so closed in
trapped like an animal
treated like an animal
feeling like an animal

trapped in a land
of no chance
as I've heard it expressed
so many times before

So sad, so sad
the tears still so easily come
to my eyes at the thought of all this
trapped in a land of no chance or opportunity
no beauty that I can see that I would love

I love the ocean with its power
out of anyone's control
as it moves
as it wishes
the best and worst things
have happened to me there:
hit for the first time
made love for the first time
had my first wedding
will probably die here

The Purple Sun — Lori Jean Finnila

I can bring new happiness to myself here
conjuring with its power
allowing it to take me over, this new place,
this new place of hope

I can dream of a new home
with peace and freedom
I can take beautiful photos
as I've dreamed of
if God will allow for me to make it here
and hopefully over and over again

It's about women who have courage
to die for their dreams

Why focus on the women
who have been hurt in some way?
How would I get through my day?
How would I know I'm not alone?
How would I have known
maybe I am one of the ones

who will get past this this time?

*When we have the strength
to show what we've accomplished
which forces society to take us as capable
individuals and give us the respect
with no heavy bearing on our bodies
that we usually have to feel everyday
when we are not at our best in this place
that helps others move forward*

*Yes you will get that second glance
at these circumstances
as long as we all continue to show
our accomplishments when we can.*

I Will Be Receiving a Long Awaited Feeling of Love

I will be awaited receiving a long feeling of love and confidence
I have so needed to give myself
I never thought I would see this day
I can't believe I can see my dreams so clear

Learning to love the body once traumatized
coming to terms with marks up and down
vertically
It lays back so eloquently now
like in a book of myths
running so many years
to be able to reflect temporarily

Astonishment and power
creating a constant change

*in physicality right before the eyes
the wings are made and begin to fly.*

Closing

'I hope this book has found you a place where you feel no shame or guilt in your life, whatever that may be. I hope you will find fulfillment in life as we all should but knowingly how hard the walls are put up to this. In all there will be beauty no matter what.'

Lori writes books for self improvement to strength, expression, and endurance for others. She captures her life as well as others to create her poems and has God beside her.

www.ingramcontent.com/pod-product-compliance
Lightning Source LLC
Chambersburg PA
CBHW051954290426
44110CB00015B/2239